Katie Woo's Crazy Critter Jokes

Based on characters created by Fran Manushkin

edited by Blake Hoena

illustrated by Tammie Lyon

PICTURE WINDOW BOOKS
a capstone imprint

Katie Woo is published by Picture Window Books,
A Capstone Imprint
1710 Roe Crest Drive
North Mankato, Minnesota 56003
www.mycapstone.com

Cataloging-in-Publication Data is available on the Library of Congress website.

ISBN: 978-1-5158-0971-5 (library binding)
ISBN: 978-1-5158-0975-3 (paperback)
ISBN: 978-1-5158-0987-6 (eBook PDF)

Summary: Katie Woo has enjoyed lots of funny animal adventures, so naturally, she knows a few great animal jokes, too. Laugh along with Katie's collection of animal knock-knocks, riddles, and more. Katie also includes tips on telling jokes.

Designer: Kayla Dohmen

Printed and bound in the United States of America.
010422R

Table of Contents

Punny **PUPPY** Jokes

What do you call a frozen puppy?

A PUP-sicle.

And what do you call a frozen dog?

A chili-dog.

What did the dog say to his classmate?

"Can you help me with my homework? I ate mine."

What type of dog can tell time?

A watch-dog.

Katie: I hear your dog plays an instrument.

Pedro: Yeah, the trom-BONE!

What do you call a dog with a high fever?

A hot dog.

**Did you hear about the dog
that swallowed a clock?**

It got ticks.

**Where did the dog
leave his car?**

In the BARKING lot!

My mom told me not to
go outside because it was raining
cats and dogs. I think she was afraid
I might step in a poodle.

HORSING
Around Jokes

Why do cowboys ride horses?

Because they are too heavy to carry.

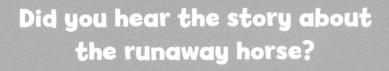

Did you hear the story about the runaway horse?

It was a tale of WHOA.

Katie: What do you call a scary horse?

Pedro: I don't know.

Katie: A night-MARE!

Why did the horse get kicked out of the barn?

It had bad STABLE manners.

What did the doctor give the pony to make it feel better?

Cough stirrup!

What did the doctor say to the sick pony?

"You're a little horse."

What did the cowgirl say after her horse fell down?

"Come on, giddy-up!"

What did the papa horse say when his pony was misbehaving?

"Quit FOALING around!"

When does a horse go out to graze?

WHINNY wants to.

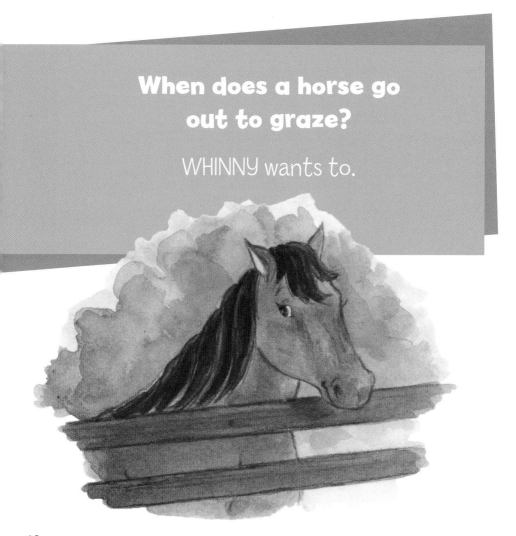

What did the momma horse say to her pony when it was getting late?

"It's PASTURE bedtime!"

I tried being friends with a horse once, but I think it had a bad attitude. Every time I asked it to play, it said, "Neigh! Neigh!"

Purr-fect **KITTY** Jokes

Did you hear the story about the cat that got into an accident?

It was a CAT-astrophe!

What do cats do after a fight?

HISS and make up.

What kind of cars do cats drive?

CAT-illacs.

What's a cat's favorite color?

PURR-ple.

Why don't any of the other animals trust the cat?

Because it was a LION.

How do cats get what they want?

Through PURR-suasion.

Why didn't any of the other animals want to play games with the cat?

Because it was a CHEETAH.

Why did the cat cross the road?

To catch the chicken.

Knock, knock. Who's there?

Catsup. Catsup who?

Catsup in a tree.

Can you get him down for me?

Did you hear about the tiger that threatened to eat all the other animals?

It was just a KITTEN.

Why do cats read the newspaper?

To catch up on the MEWS.

What do you call a pile of kittens?

A MEOW-tain.

BARNYARD
Gut-Busters

Where do cows go to have fun?

The MOO-vies.

Why did the cow cross the road?

To get to the UDDER side.

What do you call a grumpy cow?

MOO-dy.

Why did the rooster cross the road twice?

To prove he wasn't a chicken.

Where do sheep go to get a haircut?

The BAA-BAA shop.

Did you hear the story about the peacock?

It was a beautiful TALE.

What did the vet give the sick pig?

An OINK-ment.

We're sure having some fowl weather today.

Why? Is it raining geese and ducks?

Knock, knock. Who's there?
Goat. Goat who?
**GOAT open the barn door so
the cows can get out.**

What do you call a sheep that's covered in chocolate?

A candy BAAAH.

What time does a duck wake up?

The QUACK of dawn.

How do you fit more pigs on your farm?

Build a STY-scraper.

Once, I told a duck a joke, and it quacked up.

Kidding **CRITTER** Jokes

Why did the guinea pig say "Moo"?

It was trying to learn a different language.

What did the beaver say to the tree?

"Nice GNAWING you!"

What's a shark's favorite sandwich?

Peanut butter and jellyfish.

Did you hear the story about the brave fish?

It was a WHALE of a tale.

Why won't a shrimp share its toys?

Because it's shellfish.

What is a mouse's favorite game?

Hide and SQUEAK.

Why did the mouse take a bath?

It wanted to get SQUEAKY clean.

Did you hear the story about the daring rabbit?

It was a HARE-raising tale.

HOW
TO TELL A
JOKE

Even the funniest jokes can get groans if you don't tell them right. Here are my best joke-telling tips!

Know your audience— Everybody has a different sense of humor. That means different things make different people laugh. My friends like jokes about school and gross things. My grandparents think jokes about old stuff are a hoot. So I pick jokes that my audience is sure to laugh at.

by Katie Woo

Know your material—I memorize my jokes. I like to stand in front of a mirror and practice the joke until I know it by heart. That way I know I'll do a good job when I'm ready to tell it to someone.

Timing—Most jokes have two parts. The setup says what the joke is about, and the punch line is the funny part. Here's an example:

Setup: What do you call a pile of kittens?
Punch line: A MEOW-tain.

After I say the setup, I'm always excited to blurt out the punch line right away. But I stop myself. Instead, I take a deep breath and slowly count "one-banana, two-banana" in my head. That way my audience has time to think about the joke. If they don't answer by two-banana, then I shout the punch line. Ha!

Katie Woo's
stories keep the laughs going!

Keep Dancing, Katie

Katie Woo, Super Scout

The Best Club

Katie's Spooky Sleepover

THE FUN DOESN'T STOP HERE!

Discover more at www.capstonekids.com

- Videos & Contests
- Games & Puzzles
- Friends & Favorites
- Authors & Illustrators

Find cool websites and more books like this one at www.facthound.com.
Just type in the Book ID:

9781515809715

and you're ready to go!